ONE DIRECTION
Poster Book

Dear Chantelle, Happy B'day!
Love from Christina & kids
x.

:)

www.alligatorbooks.co.uk

©2013 Alligator Books
Published in 2013 by Alligator Books
Gadd House, Arcadia Avenue, London N3 2JU
The Alligator logo is a registered trade mark of Alligator Books.
Printed in China.

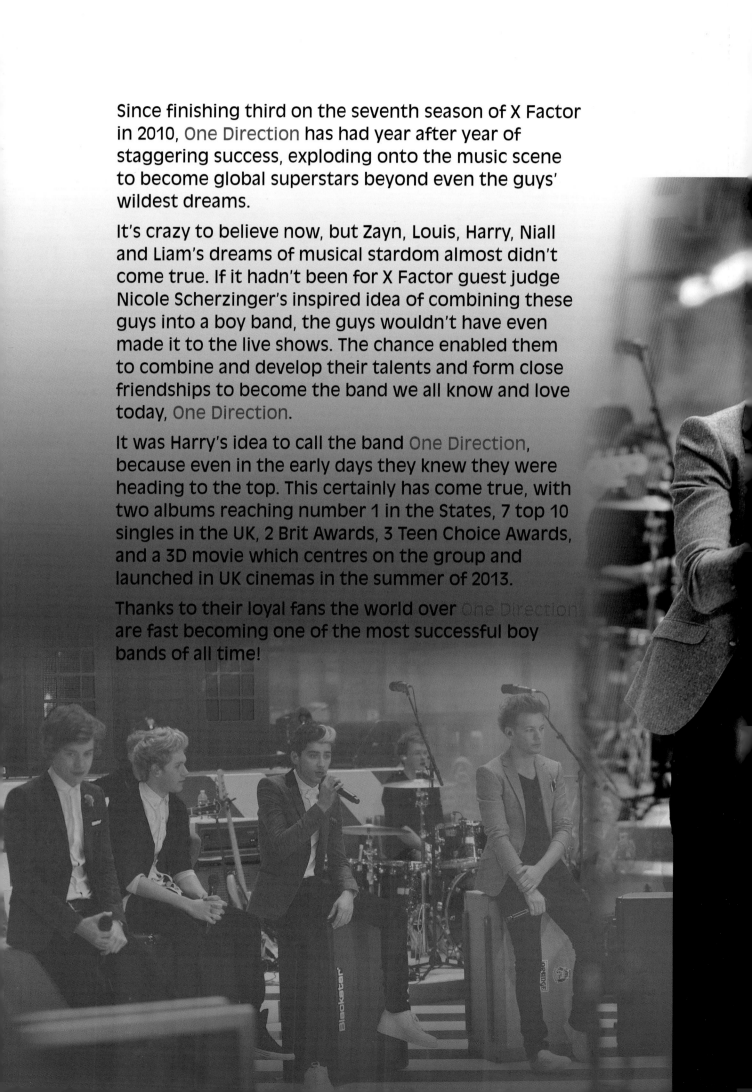

Since finishing third on the seventh season of X Factor in 2010, One Direction has had year after year of staggering success, exploding onto the music scene to become global superstars beyond even the guys' wildest dreams.

It's crazy to believe now, but Zayn, Louis, Harry, Niall and Liam's dreams of musical stardom almost didn't come true. If it hadn't been for X Factor guest judge Nicole Scherzinger's inspired idea of combining these guys into a boy band, the guys wouldn't have even made it to the live shows. The chance enabled them to combine and develop their talents and form close friendships to become the band we all know and love today, One Direction.

It was Harry's idea to call the band One Direction, because even in the early days they knew they were heading to the top. This certainly has come true, with two albums reaching number 1 in the States, 7 top 10 singles in the UK, 2 Brit Awards, 3 Teen Choice Awards, and a 3D movie which centres on the group and launched in UK cinemas in the summer of 2013.

Thanks to their loyal fans the world over One Direction are fast becoming one of the most successful boy bands of all time!

ONE DIRECTION

Harry

FAVOURITE

BAND/ARTIST The Beatles, Adele, Queen, Foster the People, Kings of Leon, Coldplay

FILMS Love Actually, Titanic, The Notebook

TV SHOW Family Guy

COLOUR Orange and Blue

FOOD Tacos, Sweetcorn, Apple Juice, T.G.I.Fridays, Chocolate HobNobs

AFTERSHAVE CK In 2U, Diesel Fuel For Life, Bleu de Chanel

THINGS!

LIKES Long Showers, Tattoos (he has over 30!), Massages, Manchester United

DISLIKES Mayonnaise, Beetroot, White Cars

PERFECT DATE Dinner and a movie

IDEAL GIRLFRIEND Non-smoker / non-swearers who wear pink and don't complain about their weight. Good sense of humour. Blue eyes.

IF HE WASN'T IN 1D Harry would want to be at university

ONE MAD FACT Harry bites two Twix bars at the same time because he doesn't want one to feel lonely

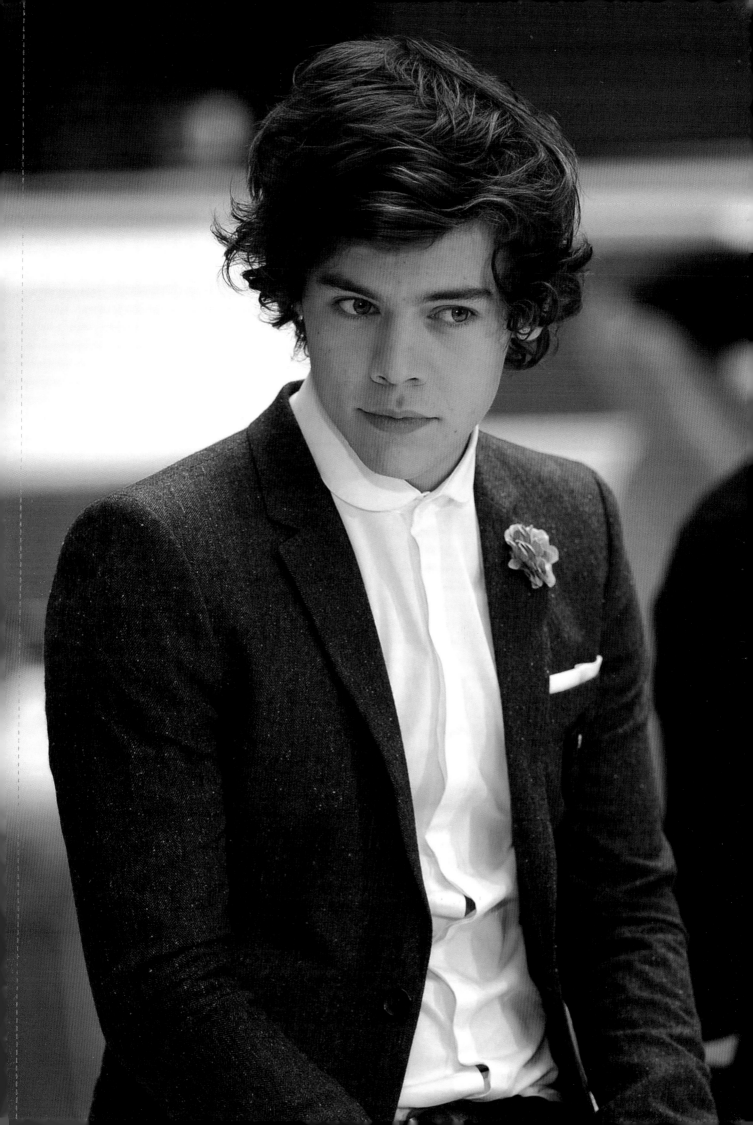

Liam

FAVOURITE

BAND/ARTIST   Jay Z, Kanye West, Ed Sheeran, Passenger, *NSYNC

FILMS   The Toy Story films (He cried watching Toy Story 3 and
                     Marley and Me)

TV SHOW   Friends

COLOUR   Purple

FOOD   Maltesers, Coca Cola, Cheeseburgers

AFTERSHAVE   Paco Rabanne's 1 million

THINGS!

LIKES   Basketball, Cooking, Boxing, Turtles, Tattoos

DISLIKES   Bullies (he used to get bullied at school), Swearing,
                     Burping, Bling

PERFECT DATE   Sitting in the back of a movie theatre or walking in a park

IDEAL GIRLFRIEND Shy, cheeky girls. Nice eyes. Quiet. Friendly. Curly hair

IF HE WASN'T IN 1D Liam would want to work in a factory building aeroplanes or
                     become a property developer

ONE MAD FACT   Because of Liam's fear of spoons, he eats ice-cream with a fork

The Music

The year 2012 was a landmark for One Direction, becoming not only a huge success in the UK but managing to conquer America too. Their first UK headlining Up All Night Tour proved so popular with fans that their growing international fan base demanded they extend their tour globally. They were also honoured with the opportunity to perform their smash hit debut single What Makes You Beautiful in front of a world audience at the closing ceremony of the London Olympic Games in 2012, where they represented the best of the UK.

Shortly after, in November, One Direction released their second album Take Me Home. The album's debut single, Live While We're Young, hit number 3 in the UK and US charts and recorded the highest first week sales for an international act in US history.

The album's second single, Little Things, debuted simultaneously with the release of the album in the UK, where both album and single topped the charts, making One Direction the youngest act in British Chart history to do so. The album was also a mega success internationally, topping the charts in more than 34 countries worldwide including the US where the album sold a staggering 540,000 in its first week. A third single from the album, Kiss You, was released in January 2013, becoming the band's sixth top 10 hit in the UK and Ireland.

In February 2013, One Direction were honoured with the chance to release the Official Comic Relief Single, One Way Or Another (Teenage Kicks). The charity single topped the charts in the UK and Ireland, becoming the bands third UK number one single. The same month the band performed the single at the 2013 Brit Awards where they were also honoured with the newly created Global Success Award showcasing their phenomenal international success and stardom. The band then embarked on their second world tour running from February to October 2013, consisting of over 100 live shows. Along with the tour, 2013 will be a big year for One Direction with the release of their first film, a 3D biopic was released in the cinemas in the summer of 2013, entitled, This Is Us.

With a loyal base of passionate fans the world over and a driven commitment to turn their dreams into a reality, expect many more great things from One Direction in the years to come.

FAVOURITE

BAND/ARTIST	Bruno Mars, Chris Brown, Urban Music, *NSYNC
FILMS	Scarface
TV SHOW	Family Guy
COLOUR	Electric Blue and Red
FOOD	Chicken, Nando's, Red Bull, Samosas, Spaghetti Bolognese
AFTERSHAVE	Unforgivable by Sean John

THINGS!

LIKES	Harry Potter, Reading, Lions, Manchester United, Tattoos
DISLIKES	People who chew loudly, Messiness
PERFECT DATE	Going out for a meal, the cinema and home to chill with some drinks
IDEAL GIRLFRIEND	Zayn's very attracted to girls' eyes (whatever the colour), Intelligent girls, Someone he can spoil, Curvy girls, Girls who play hard to get
IF HE WASN'T IN 1D	Zayn would want to be an English teacher
ONE MAD FACT	Zayn has a strange pre-gig superstition – brushing his teeth before going on stage

LOUIS

FAVOURITE

BAND/ARTIST   Ed Sheeran, The Fray, James Morrison, The Killers

FILMS   Grease, Forrest Gump

TV SHOW   Misfits, One Tree Hill

COLOUR   Dark Red

FOOD   Marmite, Pasta, Cookie Dough dessert from Pizza Hut

GROOMING PRODUCT   Dry Shampoo

THINGS!

LIKES   Manchester United, Tennis, Partying, Tattoos
                       Shoes (chinos and Toms)

DISLIKES   Baked Beans, People who chew their food too loudly, Birds

PERFECT DATE   Going to a theme park

IDEAL GIRLFRIEND   Girls who eat carrots, Girls who wear glasses (real or not),
                       Confident, Good sense of humour

IF HE WASN'T IN 1D Louis would want to train to be a Drama Teacher

ONE MAD FACT   Louis's band mates say he sleepwalks and apparently he
                       is the *messiest* of the five

Niall

FAVOURITE

BAND/ARTIST   Frank Sinatra, Bon Jovi, Coldplay, Michael Bublé, The Script

FILMS   Grease, Horror Movies, He cried at Finding Nemo

TV SHOW   Two and a Half Men

COLOUR   Green (He also likes Blue)

FOOD   Nando's, Pizza , Japanese, Italian, Chinese, Terry's Chocolate Orange

AFTERSHAVE   Armani Mania

THINGS!

LIKES   Food, Derby County Football Club, Singing in the shower, Giraffes

DISLIKES   The Only Way Is Essex

PERFECT DATE   Something fun and crazy, like going to a theme park

IDEAL GIRLFRIEND   Girls with brown eyes, Shy girls, Girls who can speak different languages and speak in different accents, Intelligent girls, Girls who don't wear make-up

IF HE WASN'T IN 1D   Niall would want to be a sound engineer

ONE MAD FACT   Niall is a natural brunette but has been dying his hair since the age of 12

ONE DIRECTION

The boys also star in a 3D biopic film centring on the group. It is called This Is Us and outlines their rapid rise to fame, from their humble hometown beginnings and competing in the X Factor, to conquering the world and performing at London's famous O2 Arena. A must-see for all fans!

"A dream is only a dream … until you decide to make it real", says Harry. One Direction have certainly seen their dreams become reality … We can't wait to see which dreams become real next for these talented guys.

We love you, One Direction!